HEALING BY FAITH
A DIVINE INTERVENTIONAL
SCRIPTURE GUIDE

HEALING BY FAITH
A DIVINE INTERVENTIONAL
SCRIPTURE GUIDE

SANDRA CALLOWAY-FIELDS

Glimpse of Glory
CHRISTIAN BOOK PUBLISHING

Dedication

This book is dedicated to all women.

Contents

Acknowledgments

To my Savior, Jesus Christ:
I would like to give thanks to my Savior, Jesus Christ. I thank You for giving me the courage to write this book.

To my husband:
Peter Fields, I thank you for being who you are in my life. Your love toward me is unconditional.

To my daughters and grandson:
I would like to thank Jania Washington and Monique Washington. You both hold a special place in my heart. I love each of you. I am grateful to be your mother. I am thankful for my grandson, Montell Washington. You are such a joy in my life. I love you.

To my parents:
I would like to thank my parents, John and Martha Calloway, for always being there for me. I appreciate you both for raising me to be the great woman that I have become.

To my siblings:
I would like to thank my brothers and their wives, David and Tracy Lee and Earnest and Kristy Calloway, and also my brother, Flozell Lee. I would also like to thank my god sister, Anita Cunningham.

To my nieces and nephews:
I would like to thank my nieces, Anissa, Diamond, Jade, Jessica, Jasmine, Janay, Joycelyn, Karen and Kamille and Shannon. I would also like to thank my nephews, Christian, Joshua, Aaron and Caleb. You all are a blessing in my life.

To a close friend:
I thank you, Jennifer, for being such a great friend. You have been there for me during some of the toughest of times.

To my pastor and first lady:
I want to thank Pastor Samuel L. Stallings and First Lady Teresa Stallings for being great, spiritual leaders in my life. I have grown spiritually since I have been under your leadership.

To my inspiration:
I thank you, Yolanda Nickerson, for being an inspiration in my life.

To my prayer partner:
I thank you, Louise White, for being my prayer partner. You are always there to pray with and for me, and I appreciate that.

Introduction

One day I was feeling so alone and lost to a busy world. I felt as if everything around me was moving so fast, and I had become drunken by its motions. My family, friends, co-workers, and church family were saying something to me, but they all seemed speechless. I could not understand exactly what they were trying to communicate to me. Something was missing, but I could not figure out what it was. I was not deaf or blind, but everyone was faceless, and their words were mute.

The pain that I was feeling in my body was unbearable. All I could do was cry out to God. I remember saying, "Lord, please help me," as the tears fell from my eyes. The room immediately became still. The calmness was so peacefully, just like my mother's embrace. The peace comforted me. Then, all of sudden, I heard a sweet, soft whisper, "Daughter, I am here with you. Do not be afraid." I immediately started feeling a tingling sensation throughout my body. I could finally rest.

The following morning, I opened my Bible to search for Scriptures to help strengthen my faith, and help others seek divine intervention. I have learned that in a day of affliction, nothing is more seasonable than prayer. Your spirit is then most humble, and your heart is broken and tender. So, it is necessary to exercise Faith and Hope under afflictions; and prayer is the appointed means to obtaining and increasing these graces.

You must stop praying for a breakthrough and accept the gift of Grace. So, what is Grace? In the New Testament in the Bible, the word "GRACE" is mentioned 156 times. It takes on a special redemptive sense in which God makes available His favor on behalf of sinners who actually do not deserve it. There is nothing you must do to receive grace. It is a gift from our Heavenly Father.

It was the grace of God that was with me the day that should have been normal for me, but turned out to be heartbreaking for me. I went into the doctor's office for my annual checkup. All the pain that I had been experiencing leading up to my appointment was about to be revealed. I was prepared to hear abnormal results due to a childhood accident. As I sat in that cold, waiting room, staring at the charts hanging on the plain white walls, the nurse came in and escorted me to the doctor's office. The doctor then revealed to me that I had cancer. Everything that he said was inaudible but the words "you have cancer." I did not know what to say or what I could do about my results. All I could do was look toward

Heaven and pray to God for comfort.

These three simple words changed my life forever: You. Have. Cancer. They still echo in my spirit to this day. There are days I just stare at my scars in the mirror and cry. I cry because "I am still here" when so many others have lost their battle to cancer. I have now found a way to cope with this disease, and it is by God's grace and mercy.

In this book, I will be sharing the A, B C'S of Faith and also Scriptures that will help strengthen you on your journey. I believe that my healing came from the help I received from the Scriptures that are shared throughout this guide.

1

Ask Jesus Christ to Heal You

If you are experiencing any form of sickness in your body, or emotional or mental distress, you have a right to ask Jesus Christ to heal you. He is able and willing to heal you completely, from the crown of your head to the soles of your feet. When God heals you, there will be no residue of the infirmity that you are dealing with right now.

God wants you to have faith that He can do it for you, before and after you ask Him to heal you. The Merriam-Webster's dictionary defines faith as "a firm belief in something for which there is no proof, something that is believed especially with strong conviction, belief and trust in and loyalty to God." Having faith is very vital! God will always respond to your faith. I encourage you to go ahead and **Ask** Him to heal you in faith.

Scriptures that will help and strengthen you:

Matthew 7:7

Keep on asking and it will be given you; keep on seeking and you will find; keep on knocking [reverently] and [the door] will be opened to you.

Hebrews 4:16

Let us then fearlessly and confidently and boldly draw near to the throne of grace (the throne of God's unmerited favor to us sinners), that we may receive mercy [for our failures] and find grace to help in good time for every need [appropriate help and well-timed help, coming just when we need it].

Psalm 121:2

My help comes from the Lord, who made heaven and earth.

John 4:10

Jesus answered her, if you had only known and had recognized God's gift and who this is that is saying to you, Give Me a drink, you would have asked Him [instead] and He would have given you living water.

John 14:13-14

And I will do [I Myself will grant] whatever you ask in My Name [as presenting all that I Am], so that the Father may be glorified and extolled in (through) the Son. [Yes] I will grant [I Myself will do for you] whatever you shall ask in My Name [as presenting all that I Am]. Children, how much more will your heavenly Father give the Holy Spirit to those who ask and continue to ask Him!

John 15:16

You have not chosen Me, but I have chosen you and I have appointed you [I have planted you], that you might go and bear fruit and keep on bearing, and that your fruit may be lasting [that it may remain, abide], so that whatever you ask the Father in My Name [as presenting all that I Am], He may give it to you.

James 1:5

If any of you is deficient in wisdom, let him ask of the giving God [Who gives] to everyone liberally and ungrudgingly, without reproaching or faultfinding, and it will be given him.

1 Peter 5:7

Casting the whole of your care [all your anxieties, all your worries, all your concerns, once and for all] on Him, for He cares for you affectionately and cares about you watchfully.

Psalm 107:28-30

Then they cry to the Lord in their trouble, and He brings them out of their distresses. He hushes the storm to a calm and to a gentle whisper, so that the waves of the sea are still. Then the men are glad because of the calm, and He brings them to their desired haven.

James 5:15

And the prayer [that is] of faith will save him who is

sick, and the Lord will restore him.

1 John 1:9

If we [freely] admit that we have sinned and confess our sins, He is faithful and just (true to His own nature and promises) and will forgive our sins [dismiss our lawlessness] and [continuously] cleanse us from all unrighteousness [everything not in conformity to His will in purpose, thought, and action].

1 John 5:14-15

And this is the confidence (the assurance, the privilege of boldness) which we have in Him: [we are sure] that if we ask anything (make any request) according to His will (in agreement with His own plan), He listens to and hears us. And if (since) we [positively] know that He listens to us in whatever we ask, we also know [with settled and absolute knowledge] that we have [granted us as our present possessions] the requests made of Him.

2

Believe That Through Jesus Christ You are Healed

According to Wikipedia, the word belief is "the state of mind in which a person thinks something to be the case, with or without there being empirical evidence to prove that something is the case with factual certainty. In other words, belief is when someone thinks something is reality, true, when they have no absolute verified foundation for their certainty of the truth or realness of something." You have to believe God for whatever it is that you need

Him to do for you, even the simple things in life. If you are not going to believe Him, then there is no point of asking Him...I asked God to heal me, and I had to believe that I was already healed. You can do the same. I encourage you to **Believe** that you are healed.

Scriptures that will help and strengthen you:

Luke 17:19

And He said to him, get up and go on your way. Your faith (your trust and confidence that spring from your belief in God) has restored you to health.

John 3:12

If you have no belief when my words are about the things of earth, how will you have belief if my words are about the things of heaven?

Mark 11:24

For this reason, I am telling you, whatever you ask for in prayer, believe (trust and be confident) that it is granted to you, and you will [get it].

John 5:39

You make search in the holy Writings, in the belief that through them you get eternal life; and it is those Writings which give witness about me.

Romans 10:17

So belief cometh of hearing, and hearing by the word of Christ.

2 Corinthians 5:7

For we walk by faith [we regulate our lives and conduct ourselves by our conviction or belief respecting man's relationship to God and divine things, with trust and holy fervor; thus we walk] not by sight or appearance.

2 Corinthians 1:24

Not that we have dominion [over you] and lord it over your faith, but [rather that we work with you as] fellow laborers [to promote] your joy, for in [your] faith (in your strong and welcome conviction or belief that Jesus is the Messiah, through whom we obtain eternal salvation in the kingdom of God) you stand firm.

Philippians 1:20

In the measure of my strong hope and belief that in nothing will I be put to shame, but that without fear, as at all times, so now will Christ have glory in my body, by life or by death.

Hebrews 12:2

Looking away [from all that will distract] to Jesus, Who is the Leader and the Source of our faith [giving the first incentive for our belief] and is also its Finisher [bringing it to maturity and perfection]. He, for the joy [of obtaining the prize] that was set before Him, endured the cross, despising and ignoring the shame, and is now seated at the right hand of the throne of God.

Psalm 103:2-5

Bless the LORD, O my soul, And forget none of His benefits; Who pardons all your iniquities, who heals all your diseases; Who redeems your life from the pit, who crowns you with loving-kindness and compassion; who satisfies your years with good things, So that your youth is renewed like the eagle.

3

Claim Your Gift in Jesus' Name

At some point in your life you may have heard your pastor or some other spiritual leader say to you or someone else, "God is going to bless you with a new house, a new car, a job promotion...He is going to restore your health, heal your body, etc." And, what they said was followed by these words: "receive it and claim it." You must understand how important it is to claim the gifts and blessings from God, even before they manifest in your life. I want you to know that your healing is nothing less than a gift from Jesus Christ. And that special gift is just what God wants you to have. I asked and prayed to God for my healing. I believed that He would heal me, but something was missing. I needed more. Then, it occurred to me that I had not claimed my healing. I knew that was important, so I immediately claimed my healing in the name of Jesus Christ. Have you claimed your healing yet? If not, I encourage you to **Claim** your healing today.

Scriptures that will help and strengthen you:

Isaiah 44:7

Who is like me? Let him make his claim! Let him announce it and explain it to me –since I established an ancient people—let them announce future events!

2 Corinthians 3:5

By ourselves we are not qualified to claim that anything comes from us. Rather, our credentials come from God.

Isaiah 55:6

Seek, inquire for, and require the Lord while He may be found [claiming Him by necessity and by right]; call upon Him while He is near.

Amos 5:14

Pursue good and not evil, so that you may live, and this is what will happen: The LORD God of the Heavenly Armies will be with you, as you have been claiming.

Haggai 1:8

Go up to the hill country and bring lumber and rebuild [My] house, and I will take pleasure in it and

I will be glorified, says the Lord [by accepting it has done for My glory and by displaying My glory in it].

John 5:44

How can you believe? While accepting glory from one another, you don't seek the glory that comes from the only God.

Ephesus 4:2

With all humility and gentleness, with patience, accepting one another in love.

John 3:16

For God so greatly loved and dearly prized the world that He [even] gave up His only begotten (unique) Son, so that whoever believes in (trusts in, clings to, relies on) Him shall not perish (come to destruction, be lost) but have eternal (everlasting) life.

4

Declare Your Faith

The Merriam-Webster's dictionary defines faith as "a firm belief in something for which there is no proof, something that is believed especially with strong conviction, belief and trust in and loyalty to God." I had to find my faith in the midst of my crisis. When I was diagnosed with cancer, I was very angry. I did not want anyone to feel pity for me because this was my journey.

I had to go through the asking, believing and claiming God's grace to get to where I am in my life right now. I remember asking God how much longer

I would have to deal with cancer because it was a heavy load for me. I knew I had to declare my faith, and it was much more than my belief in God. It gave me the ability to fight even harder. You see, I now realize that sometimes in life you have to push your way through everything to get to God. I encourage you to activate your **Faith** in this season of your life.

Scriptures that will help and strengthen you:

<u>2 Corinthians 12:9</u>

But He said to me, my grace (My favor and loving-kindness and mercy) is enough for you [sufficient against any danger and enables you to bear the trouble manfully]; for My strength and power are made perfect (fulfilled and completed) and show themselves most effective in [your] weakness. Therefore, I will all the more gladly glory in my weaknesses and infirmities, that the strength and power of Christ (the Messiah) may rest (yes, may pitch a tent over and dwell) upon me!

Philippians 4:19

And my God will liberally supply (fill to the full) your every need according to His riches in glory in Christ Jesus.

James 5:14

Is anyone among you sick? He should call in the church elders (the spiritual guides). And they should pray over him, anointing him with oil in the Lord's name.

Deuteronomy 4:4

But you who kept faith with the Lord are living,

every one of you today.

Joshua 23:14

Now I am about to go the way of all the earth: and you have seen and are certain, all of you, in your hearts and souls, that in all the good things which the Lord said about you, he has kept **faith** with you; everything has come true for you.

2 Sam 22:31

As for God, his way is all good: the word of the Lord is tested; he is a safe cover for all those who put their **faith** in him.

Job 39:11

Will you put your **faith** in him, because his strength is great? Will you give the fruit of your work into his care?

Mark 5:25-29

And there was a woman who had had a flow of blood for twelve years, and who had endured much suffering under [the hands of] many physicians and had spent all that she had, and was no better but instead grew worse. She had heard the reports concerning Jesus, and she came up behind Him in the throng and touched His garment, For she kept saying, If I only touch His garments, I shall be restored to health. And immediately her flow of blood was dried up at the source, and [suddenly] she felt in her body that she was healed of her [distressing] ailment.

Mark 5:34

And He said to her, Daughter, your faith (your trust and confidence in Me, springing from faith in God) has restored you to health. Go in (into) peace and be continually healed and freed from your [distressing bodily] disease.

5

Effectual Fervent Prayer

The Word of the Lord says, "And there was a woman who had a flow of blood for twelve years, and who had endured much suffering under [the hands of] many physicians and had spent all that she had, and was no better but instead grew worse. She had heard the reports concerning Jesus, and she came up behind Him in the throng."

Before I could move any further in my healing process, I had to understand how to pray, and also the meaning and importance of effectual fervent prayers. I had to study both words, effectual and fervent. The Merriam-Webster's dictionary defines the word effectual as "producing a desired result or effect." The word fervent means "felt very strongly." Now when I pray, I feel very strongly about my desired results. I encourage you to start praying **Effectual Fervent** prayers.

Scriptures that will help and strengthen you:

Rom 15:30

Now I urge you, brothers and sisters, through our Lord Jesus Christ and through the love of the Spirit, to join fervently with me in prayer to God on my behalf.

Psalm 17:6

I call upon you, for you will answer me, God. Listen

closely to me and hear my prayer.

Psalm 54:2

Hear my prayer, O God; give ear to the words of my mouth.

Psalm39:12

Hear my prayer, O LORD, and give ear unto my cry; hold not thy peace at my tears: for I am a stranger with thee, and a sojourner, as all my fathers were.

Psalm 69:13

O Lord, may you hear my prayer and be favorably disposed to me! O God, because of your great loyal love, answer me with your faithful deliverance!

Psalm 86:6

Lord, hear my prayer; listen to my plea for mercy.

Psalm 102:1

A prayer of the afflicted, when he is overwhelmed, and poureth out his complaint before the Lord! Hear my prayer, O Lord and let my cry come unto thee.

1 Kings 8:28

Jehovah my God, I am your servant. Listen to my prayer. Grant the requests I make to you today.

Psalm 54:2

God, listen to my prayer, and pay attention to the words of my mouth.

2 Chronicles 6:20

Day and night may your eyes be on this Temple, the place where you said your name will be. Listen to me as I pray toward this place.

Psalm 17:6

I call to you for you will answer me, O God. Listen to me! Hear what I say!

James 5:16

Confess your faults one to another, and pray one for another, that you may be healed. The effectual fervent prayer of a righteous man avails much.

6

Find Your Purpose

I could hear the sweet voice of God telling me that I was not finish and that I had a purpose to fulfill. I thought to myself, "What purpose and how could I find it?" I wanted others to define my purpose and validate it. As a young girl, I was told I was a caregiver. So I begin to care for others, and taking on that responsible was a great task. The day I was diagnosed with cancer, I thought that I could take care of myself. I was wrong. I really needed help, but I did not know how to seek help. I searched online for information and I asked my doctors. I felt alone while searching for help.

While seeking help, I could hear the voice of God saying, "Don't give up." The question still remained, "how could I find my purpose, if I could not find anyone to help me?" At that moment, it was clear that my purpose is to help others who are battling with the disease called cancer. I am excited about executing my purpose. I encourage you to seek God about your **Purpose** in life. "May he give you your heart's desire, and put all your **purposes** into effect."

Scriptures that will help and strengthen you:

Exodus 9:16

However, I have let you live for this purpose: to show you My power and to make My name known in all the earth.

Deuteronomy 29:12

With the purpose of taking part in the agreement of the Lord your God, and his oath which he makes with you today:

Romans 11:33

O the depth of the riches, and of the wisdom, and of the knowledge of God! How unsearchable are his purposes, and his ways past finding out!

Ecclesiastes 3:1

For everything there is a season, and a **time for every purpose under heaven**:

2 Corinthians 9:7

Each one must do just as he has purposed in his heart, not grudgingly or under compulsion, for God loves a cheerful giver.

2 Timothy 3:10

Now you followed my teaching, conduct, purpose, faith, patience, love, perseverance

Job 22:28

Your purposes will come about, and light will be shining on your ways.

Psalm 20:4

May he give you your heart's desire, and put all your purposes into effect.

7

Gaining Favor

I thought after I found my purpose I was finished. And then I quickly realized that I needed favor. What is favor and how can we obtain it? The Merriam-Webster's dictionary defines favor as "a kind or helpful act that you do for someone; approval, support or popularity; preference for one person, group, etc. over another." God is the One who will grant any of us favor.

He has shown me so much favor over the years. I haven't had to go through this process alone. He has opened doors for me, put the right people around me and even made provision for me since I was diagnosed with cancer. Now that's favor. He will also give you favor too, with Him and with others. I encourage you to ask and believe God that He will grant you with **Favor** as you continue on your journey.

Scriptures that will help and strengthen you:

Genesis 6:8
Noah, however, found favor in the eyes of the Lord.

Genesis 26:24
And the Lord appeared to him the same night and said, I am the God of Abraham your father. Fear not, for I am with you and will favor you with blessings and multiply your descendants for the sake of My servant Abraham.

Exodus 33:13

Now if I have indeed found favor in Your sight, please teach me Your ways, and I will know You and find favor in Your sight. Now consider that this nation is Your people."

Leviticus 26:9

For I will be leaning toward you with favor and regard for you, rendering you fruitful, multiplying you, and establishing and ratifying My covenant with you.

Numbers 6:26

The Lord looks with favor on you and gives you peace.

Philippians 3:8

Yes, furthermore, I count everything as loss compared to the possession of the priceless privilege (the overwhelming preciousness, the surpassing worth, and supreme advantage) of knowing Christ Jesus my Lord and of progressively becoming more deeply and intimately acquainted with Him [of perceiving and recognizing and understanding Him more fully and clearly]. For His sake I have lost everything and consider it all to be mere rubbish (refuse, dregs), in order that I may win (gain) Christ (the Anointed One),

Philippians 1:29

For you have been given the privilege for the Messiah's sake not only to believe in him but also to suffer for him.

8

Healing for Your Mind and Body

With my diagnoses of cancer, I had to have 30 radiation treatments. Every time I went into the doctor's office for my treatments, I felt nauseated and weak. I would even vomit during the course of my radiation treatments. My body was so weak and my muscles ached. I felt miserable during and after the entire 30 treatments. I felt like my health was failing. I also felt like I was losing at one point, but God released His peace upon my life. He assured me that I was strong, even on the days I felt weak.

I want you to know that whatever sickness you

are facing at this point in your life, God will use it for His Glory. You may feel like you are losing too, but you are actually winning because Jesus is right with you, just like He has been with me. He hasn't forgotten about you. He will give you a peace of mind and the strength in your body to keep moving forward. I encourage you to believe that there is healing for your **Mind** and **Body**, and it is released from Heaven. Isaiah 53:5 declares that you (we) are healed by Jesus' stripes.

Scriptures that will help and strengthen you:

Proverbs 16:24

Pleasant words are as a honeycomb, sweet to the mind and healing to the body.

Romans 8:6

For the mindset of the flesh [is] death, but the mindset of the Spirit [is] life and peace.

Romans 8:27

And the one who searches our hearts knows what the mindset of the Spirit [is], because he intercedes on behalf of the saints according to [the will of] God.

Deuteronomy 4:29

But if from there you will seek (inquire for and require as necessity) the Lord your God, you will find Him if you [truly] seek Him with all your heart [and mind] and soul and life.

Deuteronomy 6:5

You must love the Lord your God with your whole mind, your whole being, and all your strength.

Deuteronomy 26:16

This day the Lord your God has commanded you to do these statutes and ordinances. Therefore, you shall keep and do them with all your [mind and] heart and with all your being.

Deuteronomy 30:6

The Lord your God will also cleanse your heart and the hearts of your descendants so that you may love him with all your mind and being and so that you may live.

Deuteronomy 30:14

For the thing is very near you -- it is in your mouth and in your mind so that you can do it.

Colossians 3:23

Whatever you do, work at it wholeheartedly as though you were doing it for the Lord and not merely for people.

9

Incredible God

Every day I recognize how incredible God is. He comforts me. He holds me close to Him. He motivates me to keep going. He has given my life purpose. He has expanded my knowledge, wisdom and understanding. He has lifted my soul. He has helped me see how important I am and how my life matters. He has healed me. Even though I have not received the full manifestation of my healing, I have no doubt received it and claimed it, in the Mighty name of Jesus.

I know that if you would be honest with yourself, you will be able to share just how incredible God is to you too. Didn't He keep your mind in the midst of your storm? Didn't He lift your spirit when you were feeling low some days? Hasn't He been a friend during the times no one was even available for you when you needed them? Hasn't He showed up at every doctor's appointment? Hasn't He provided every one of your needs? Hasn't He been good to you? I encourage you to stay in the presence of God, and know that you can always talk to Him, no matter what hour of the day it is.

Scriptures that will help and strengthen you:

1 John 3:1

See what [an incredible] quality of love the Father has given (shown, bestowed on) us, that we should [be permitted to] be named and called and counted the children of God! And so we are! The reason that the world does not know (recognize, acknowledge) us is that it does not know (recognize, acknowledge) Him.

John 6:62

"Does this seem incredible to you? What then if you were to see the Son of Man ascending again where He was before?

Ephesians 1:19

And what is the surpassing greatness of His power toward us who believe. These are in accordance with the working of the strength of His might.

Isaiah 14:27

"For the Lord of hosts has planned, and who can

frustrate it? And as for His stretched-out hand, who can turn it back?"

Luke 1:37

"For nothing will be impossible with God."

Jeremiah 32:27

"Behold, I am the Lord, the God of all flesh; is anything too difficult for Me?"

Deuteronomy 33:27

"The eternal God is a dwelling place, And underneath are the everlasting arms; And He drove out the enemy from before you, And said, 'Destroy!'

Psalm 65:6

The One who established the mountains by his strength is clothed with omnipotence.

Exodus 15:2

Jehovah is my strong defender. He is the one who has saved me. He is my God, and I will praise him, my father's God, and I will sing about his greatness.

Psalm 118:28

You are my God, and I give you thanks. I will proclaim your greatness.

A Personal Message from the Author

I hope and pray that this book has touched and blessed your life in some special way. And my desire for you is that God will continue blessing every area of your life. I encourage you to continue smiling and being hopeful and confident that our Lord, Jesus Christ, will completely heal you. I would be remiss if I don't tell you to remain humble as the Word of God encourages us to do in Proverbs 16:19, "Better it is to be of an humble spirit with the lowly, than to divide the spoil with the proud."

My grandson, Montell, gives me so many reasons to smile everyday. He is one of my biggest motivators and reasons to keep pushing toward my destiny.

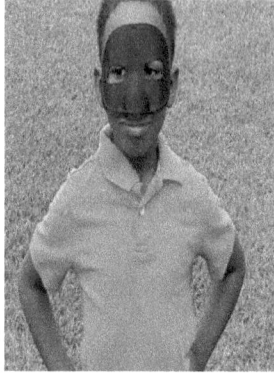

PERSONAL JOURNAL

*

*

*

*

*

*

*

*

*

*

*

*

*

*

*

*

*

*

*

*

*

*

*

*

*

*

*

*

*

*

*

*

*

*

*